©2008, Michelle Kabele. All rights reserved. No part of this publication may be reproduced without written permission of the author.

ISBN 9780982068601
Library of Congress Control Number: 2008936458

TABLE OF CONTENTS

Introduction 3

Chapter 1: Yes, It Is Your Job! 7

The Manufacturer's Role and Why It Matters 8
Good Marketing Tactics Work. Better Tactics Make You Successful 9
10 Tips for Identifying New Opportunities With Your Existing Clients . 10

Chapter 2: Get To Know Your Customer 16

Rule #1 – Offer your customers something of value that they can't get
anywhere else. 18
Rule #2 – Make a list of 20 questions to ask your 10 key customers . . . 19
10 Ways To Use Your Database To Build Your Business 19

Chapter 3: Develop Your Database 22

10 Low-Cost/No-Cost Marketing Ideas 23
Start With the Right Software 24
Build a Better Database 25
Why Your Database Will Give *You* the Competitive Edge 26

**Chapter 4: Changing Channels: Rethink Your
Marketing Options** 29

Preparing Your Marketing Mix 31
Ingredients in the Mix 32

Chapter 5: Unraveling the Web 36

K.I.S.S. – Keep It Simple, Stupid 37
Generating Leads from the Web 38
10 Ways to Maximize Your Website's Value 39

Chapter 6: Plan for Success 44

What Does a Great Marketing Plan Accomplish? 46
The Marketing Assessment 46
Determine Your Marketing Budget 45

Chapter 7: Measure Your Progress 50

How Do You Know What Works? 51
Balancing Creativity With Results 52

Summary 56

⬤ Introduction

Remember how your mother, teacher, or that wise old man inside your head kept telling you "nothing in life is free?" Sure, you also hear that there's no free ride and no such thing as a free lunch, and you get what you pay for. Well, I'm here to tell you that all those platitudes are not exactly true.

Great marketing *is* free! And if you don't seize the opportunity to drive your business with this knowledge, then you're already falling behind — because I can assure you that at least one of your competitors is taking advantage of what I'm about to share with you.

So take a seat and hold on tight. Throughout these pages you're going to learn how to grab your leads, databases, and market segments and get them revved up into a high performance machine. They're going to purr with power because of your new-found marketing knowledge and the tactics that you'll easily put in place, over time, without spending a dime or tapping into your bottom line. Ultimately, it's all about knowing the end user of your products — your customers — and knowing them intimately. Everyone wants to garner the benefits of word-of-mouth marketing. I'm going to show you how to put a plan into action that will have your customers coming back for more and your competitors scratching their heads to figure out how to salvage the market share you're snagging.

In today's market, to be truly successful as a reseller, you need to do more than just buy and sell. Those days are gone.

Do you remember guerilla marketing with all sorts of low cost ways to get your message into the world? Then there was Seth Godin's "Purple Cow" — remarkable on its own — telling us to be remarkable so you could stand out in the field. Now there's Godin's latest marketing wisdom, "Meatball Sundae," with a host of bloggers and consultants talking about the transformation the Web brings. Do you think these don't apply to you? Or that you can't do it? Think again – you **can**!

Consider who your market is. How do you reach them? What do they need that you're not already delivering? How could you boost their businesses with your product lines and services? And how do you communicate that — and ultimately market yourself — to your existing customers and future prospects? As a Value Added Reseller (VAR), how do you build a loyal following? Where can you capitalize to bring in new customers at the same time?

Don't answer yet. I'm going to help you find the solutions, one step at a time. All you have to do is open your mind to the possibility that your marketing could be better and it doesn't take a pile of cash. Because, let's face it, the money train isn't stopping at your station, is it?

A majority of resellers are failing or just getting by. Some say that 75 percent of VARs are insolvent or facing bankruptcy. It's not because they are bad salespeople. No, they know how to sell. But they don't know how to *market*. Big difference!! And they don't know *why* they should market. I'm guessing because you're reading this book that you're probably part of the 25 percent of resellers who are on solid ground and looking for a way to keep moving onward and upward.

Get to know your customers! Become a detective and uncover the clues to their needs — which are often unspoken. You'll be a hero when you swoop in with a smart solution that makes their jobs easier. Imagine if someone did that for you. Wouldn't your loyalty meter rise? Once you become a problem-solver instead of a vendor, you will develop long-term relationships with your customers.

And it all starts with your database...But PLEASE, don't just input your contacts and say, "There, my database is all set and if I need a phone number or a birthday, I know where to find it." Your database should be the first glimpse at the secrets of your customers. Your key to intimacy. It is more than an alphabetized list of names and phone numbers. Here is where you will find a wealth of clues to what your customers need and what they're missing. Begin to touch your database everyday. It will give you insight and offer the perception to your customers that you truly are interested in their problems and needs.

Once you have a genuine handle on your customers and how to continue to massage your database to work its best for you, you'll begin to understand where and how to apply the free marketing tactics I'm sharing in this book. Of course, there are traditional marketing channels in print, broadcast, direct mail, and telemarketing, but maybe relying on traditional marketing modes isn't going to get you ahead this time. In today's fast-paced business world, integrating traditional pieces with new technologies is the only way to succeed. And the beauty of this? Maximizing these new technologies to your advantage and then generating new leads is *virtually* free (no pun intended). With nanosecond technology and "Don't Blink" marketing that I'm going to explain, you must have your finger on the trigger at all times, keeping pace and keeping up with a dynamic, ever-changing business environment, thanks to none other than, yes, the Internet.

I'll show you how to develop an integrated marketing mix with strong Internet elements that drive your business by harnessing the power of your website. We'll explore the value of establishing, implementing and maintaining a marketing plan. "Focus" will be your new daily buzzword. Tracking your progress will help you see which initiatives are working well for you, what needs to be tweaked, and what should be shelved or scratched out of your plan completely. You'll learn to stay ahead of the latest trends, brainstorm ideas, and determine where it makes sense to place your energy to be successful.

Now, for every person who says to you, "That won't work," I challenge you to reply with "Why not?" That's how Bill Gates replied. And Steve Jobs. Ultimately, if you feel comfortable with your marketing efforts, you're failing. You need to take risks to succeed.

Remember, ideas are free. And there are lots of them – based on your experience, on the feedback from others, on knowledge – ideas that can change your business – ideas that can help your business be unique, special and add value for your customer.

It's time to dive in. Are you ready?

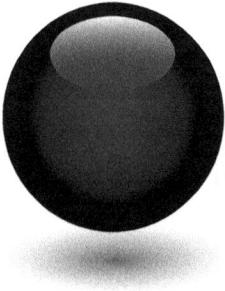

Chapter 1:
Yes, It Is Your Job!

Marketing isn't one of those tasks you can tackle when it's convenient. Marketing is a part of your job — a very important part. In today's competitive arena, dialing a phone number to say "hi" or just being an order taker making sales calls doesn't cut it. Marketing is the critical differential for businesses that will be successful versus those that will forever struggle to get by. It is vital for you to understand your role as a reseller and SuperVAR and the importance of the manufacturer's role in your success.

You must get inside the head of your customers. Figure out what their problems are. Then find a way to help solve them. You don't need an MBA to do this successfully. It doesn't require complex formulas or a marketing pyramid to get the answers. You simply have to ask your customers the right questions. Most people are eager to tell you what their problems are. And when they do, the answer will come to you— free of charge!

The Manufacturer's Role and Why It Matters

The manufacturer's role is to provide reliable products for its customers at reasonable prices. Today, manufacturers seek out VARs who will make their job easy **and** provide remarkable value for the price by doing more than just waiting for the orders to roll in. Gone are the days of long, chatty lunches, a round of 18 on the local golf course, and dinner parties with wives and friends. While you still may have business relationships that allow for these special times, customers are not as loyal as they were in the past. They are bargain hunters, **but** they insist on value.

Way back when, in the days when you first started selling, life was pretty easy. You'd grab a prospect list and, one by one, call the contacts, starting at the top and plodding along until you got to the bottom, gathering up buyers along the way. Customers were often eager — or at least curious — to meet with you to hear what new services you could provide that would make their company more profitable. You knew it all back then. You were a leading sales rep, one whom manufacturers sought out because of your talent and expertise in the field.

And then the Internet flooded your world, increasing competition and driving the demands for more and better service. No longer could you simply peddle your wares within your territory and let nature take its inevitable course. Your customers grew to expect you to be more than a supplier. They wanted a knowledgeable resource to provide consulting support for their business challenges; in other words, a SuperVAR!

Today, SuperVARs are in your territory, grabbing your business, by going beyond the norm. Your customers are still your buddies, but many are leaving you to join the ranks of your competitor's more contented customers. These buyers are now looking for a great price for your product **and** great quality and value. Plus, they want realistic solutions to their business issues. They're savvier than ever before because so much information is readily available with a couple of clicks of the mouse. Customers know, for example, that a bargain price on switches from an unauthorized dealer can cost them a bundle in the end if those parts turn out to be counterfeit. But, they'll pay considerably more to get the quality that only comes with authentic switches. That's value.

Good Marketing Tactics Work. Better Tactics Make You Successful.

So why do analysts predict that nearly 40 percent of today's VARs will soon be out of business unless they make substantial changes to their business model?[1]

Here's the deal: you **have** to market yourself! It's your job! Toot your own horn, figure out what you're great at and let the world – and of course, your customers – know! What distinguishes you from your competitors?

Define your value proposition: the characteristics or traits that lift you above all of your competitors. Then talk about it! According to Channel Media Publication's *2006 Solution Provider Marketing Research*, when you employ "good" marketing tactics like segmentation, repetition, and integrated messages, *marketing works*![1] And most of that great marketing is — you guessed it — free. When good marketing tactics

10 Tips for Identifying New Opportunities With Your Existing Clients

1. Touch your database every day. Use it. Browse it. Give yourself a specific database task, like running a report of everyone who bought a specific product in the past 12 months or a list of customers who represent a moderate spending level (so you can focus on up-selling them). Send a few emails or call some of those customers with your ideas. It will demonstrate that you're interested in your end user when you know what your customers' needs and problems are.

2. Segment your database into groups by common factors. Group customers with like business problems, figure out their major problem, and then solve it for everyone within that one group. You'll look like the hero to each customer in the whole group, while saving time, energy, and resources by solving one common problem.

3. Find the true experts for those areas of your field where are applied, you may see significant financial impact to your bottom line. There is the potential for:

- 20-25 percent increase in the number of qualified leads;
- 25-30 percent increase in sales revenue; and
- 25-30 percent increase in cross-selling/up-selling opportunities.

But, when you apply "better" marketing tactics and techniques, you may generate results that are two to three times *better* than the average VAR:

- 65-70 percent increase in the number of qualified leads;
- 70-75 percent increase in sales revenue; and
- 60-65 percent increase in cross-selling/up-selling opportunities.

Which group would YOU rather join? It's pretty clear – great marketing affects your bottom line. So what opportunities are you missing because of your own marketing myopia?

you may be a little weak. Partner with these thought leaders and utilize their knowledge in order to solve customer problems.

4. Offer your customers solutions that subtly up-sell and cross-sell for you. Discuss their spoken need and analyze their unspoken need. Then solve both.

5. About 70 to 80 percent of your sales come from existing customers so don't always look for new leads. Instead, know the potential that lies here, within your reach.

6. Follow the trends in your customers' product sales and make yourself stand out among the other resellers by having this new trend information at your fingertips. Become a trusted advisor and help them discover what's going to be hot, why some products aren't moving, and how to make improvements to push inventory.

7. Host a breakfast seminar with a guest speaker on hot topics your customers want to learn more about. Become a source of knowledge and connection for your customers.

Lead Generation – Did you know that 70 to 80 percent of a company's sales comes from existing customers? Quite simply, it costs less to reach your existing customers because you already know who they are, where they are, and what products they need. So capitalize on that knowledge.

Market Segments — Overlooking the power of market segmentation can mean the difference between an overwhelmingly successful marketing campaign and one that falls flat. Market segmentation divides your customers into clearly defined groups, with each segment possessing its own set of characteristics, behaviors, and/or needs. Going beyond merely categorizing by geographic location, market segmentation gets down to the "nuts and bolts" of what motivates people to buy: personality, attitude, interests, options, etc. Understanding those factors lets you focus your marketing programs on those customers likely to be interested in your products.

8. Partner with the event speakers to create an executive summary and landing pages for your website. Consider a webinar or podcast to reinforce the event, which will either extend the event content or reinforce it. You can provide password access to special tools for attendees and/or provide basic information for people who find you via the Web and then use the registration process to capture their contact information before providing full access.

9. Word-of-mouth – Ask your customers to bring their friends to your next exclusive customer event. Consider recording some of your customers' success stories, exploring how the solution increased their business efficiency and lowered their costs. Ask these customers to introduce the next speaker and outline how your partnership helped their business. Then post these stories on your website.

10. Look beyond product pricing and become a valuable solution provider. Therein lies the key to profitability.

Marketing Layers — Peel back that list of leads to get to the heart – here's where you'll find your greatest lead potential. Identify the key characteristics, job titles, and responsibilities of your target audience. Then pinpoint how you can meet their needs. Now you'll be targeting, and marketing, to a group with common themes, investing your time in one specific area versus the time-intensive alternative of randomly calling on 5,000 names.

Your Website and Internet Presence — Your overall marketing strategy should include a strong online presence. More than just "throwing a site up" and crossing your fingers, focus on maximizing this powerful marketing tool that can generate more leads and, ultimately, close more deals.

Partnering — Developing your own partner-to-partner network means finding the best resources for your customers and the services you provide them — whether you sub-contract the services under your own business umbrella or provide clients with the direct connection. The best partners will allow you to do everything for your customers "under one roof".

Up-selling and Cross-selling – Address the spoken *and* the unspoken needs of your customers. You will provide them with a greater service by offering solutions to their current problems and anticipating their future needs. When you include value-added add-ons to their current purchases, you ultimately avert problems that may otherwise arise later on. Regardless of the products, the opportunity to successfully up-sell and cross-sell hinges on determining what the end-user wants to accomplish.

Nanosecond Technology — Our world can literally change overnight. You must keep pace with this dynamic, global environment — but that doesn't mean you have to start from scratch. You just need to open your mind to a different methodology. Today, your strategy should look like this: Do. Do. Do. In other words, get your message out into the marketplace. Launch the new product or service now. Retool it later. If you wait, someone else will jump in and grab your market share. Or your idea will be outdated by the time it hits the market.

Create a Marketing Mix — To determine your ideal combination, start by mirroring the mindset of the people you want to reach. If they are mostly Internet-savvy customers adept at collecting information and making comparisons online, provide the immediate information they want or you risk losing sales. If they still value a face-to-face interaction, be ready to accommodate their preferences in your mix. Print, radio, email marketing, ezines, podcasts, TV, sponsorships – determine those avenues that work best for which customers, then implement a plan.

Capitalize on Missed Sales Opportunities — When properly managed, a good database gives you much more than just a list of customers and what they've bought. It speaks volumes about your own organization. I'll delve into this subject at length in Chapter 3.

Make a Plan — Determine what your customers need and those services you have that will help them fill those needs. Then craft a marketing and sales plan that incorporates solutions to their problems by capitalizing on your strengths and improving on your weaknesses. Then use your new-found sales tools to dazzle your existing customers again like you did years ago. The new leads will automatically follow.

As you can see, many of these marketing tools aren't rocket science. They just require a bit of thought, and more importantly, stepping back and reviewing the tools that you already have in your bag of tricks — and determining how you can use those tools differently and maximize information that already exists. Make your plan. Commit to implementing it. Then set aside just a few hours a week to work on it, to learn more about your existing customers and how you're going to talk to them and provide them great, valuable products and services.

[1] Channel Media Publication, *2006 Solution Provider Marketing Research*

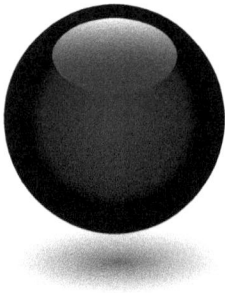

Chapter 2:
Get To Know Your Customer

Are you intimate with your customers? Do you even know how to tell?

If you are a successful VAR who offers your customers something that no other competitor does, chances are, your relationship is pretty solid. By getting to know your customer, you were able to pinpoint their needs and problems — which are often subtly expressed — and then provide the service or product that presented the solution. You got inside your customer's head – bravo! You've taken one of the initial critical steps in garnering great marketing for free: figuring out what your customers really need versus just selling them the status quo.

Getting to know your customers means sharing information as a true business partner. You must provide your customers with information and resources above and beyond the standard perception in the industry. And all you have to do is ask your customer, "What problems are you having?" and "How can I help you solve them?" Become a detective and uncover the unexpressed clues to their needs. Once you become a problem-solver instead of a vendor, you will develop long-term relationships with your customers, which translates into greater profits because you haven't had to invest as much here as you would in cultivating new customers. Think of it like dating. A new relationship requires much more effort and energy than rekindling the fires of a familiar one!

So how do you do it? How do you ask the questions? And *what* do you ask? Some of the questions are easy, like, "What is keeping you up at night?" or maybe you're working with a mid-level manager, who is solving the boss' problems and the line worker's problem at the same time — simply stuck in the middle, between that proverbial rock and a hard place. Remember, most people want to tell you what their problems are, but they prefer to be asked. It's your job to question, and then be a good listener, and *then* turn that information into solutions, and profits to your bottom line.

Rule #1 – Offer your customers something of value that they can't get anywhere else.

First, let's figure out why your existing customers order from you. If you think it's strictly your price point or availability or because your sales rep is a nice guy, think again. More likely, they come back to you again and again because you offer something of value – something intangible that they can't get anywhere else.

Let's say John Doe at XYZ Industries calls and says he'll need 1200 widgets this year but doesn't want to fork over the cash for all of them at once. You ask a simple question, "How many will you need each month?" John estimates 100 per month should be adequate, so you call the manufacturer and arrange for them to automatically ship 100 per month for a year, while also locking in the current price to avoid any hikes later in the year. Suddenly, John is happy because you've saved him the hassle of placing an order every month, John's assembly manager loves him because he doesn't have to store excessive inventory, and John's boss – who doesn't realize you're shipping them automatically – rewards John for being so "on top of things." Thanks to you, John is a hero. You have solved John's problem, making him look pretty good in the process. As a result, you solidified your relationship with the customer for some time to come. Bottom line, you got to know your customer and his needs and problems. You exceeded his expectations and you resolved his issues.

Rule #2 – Make a list of 20 questions to ask your 10 key customers.

How do you know what value your organization offers? Ask your customers! Find out what makes them tick (and ticked off).

Start by querying your database to find out which end-users are most vital to your business. They are your opinion leaders, and what they say matters. Survey those users online, by postcard or telephone. You might even consider hosting a breakfast meeting. Tell them you respect their opinions and you'd like to tap into their knowledge so that you can ultimately serve them better. Ask them why they choose to order from you instead of someone else. What key things are important to them today? Where is their business going tomorrow? What are their common concerns? What add-ons are they most interested in? Remember, it's not about offering the lowest price or the having the biggest variety of

10 Ways To Use Your Database To Build Your Business

1. Up-sell and cross-sell to existing customers and become your customer's hero by selling the solution to their problem.

2. Focus your marketing campaigns on specific segments within your customer groups.

3. Monitor sales by product or geographic distribution to see where your "hot" and "cold" customers are.

4. Spot buying trends.

5. Pinpoint high-value prospects.

6. Determine your market penetration. How many customers do you have in your target market?

7. Calculate how much of their wallet you are capturing. Are they buying their supplies and incremental purchases from you? Focus your limited resources on the customers generating the most return.

8. Create measurable retention

inventory on your shelves, because any of your competitors can come along and match that.

Once you've asked these all-important questions, **listen** to their answers. Then leverage that information to become an expert for your customers. If they want onsite support or training and you can make it happen by forming new partnerships or alliances with vendors, do it! If it's a different price structure or cooperative advertising, make it happen! Remember, if their business grows, so does yours.

programs and track their return. Utilize the information in your database to send customized notes to your best clients (special dates, such as when to call for a follow-up, the last time you held a business review with them, etc.) This not only builds a retention program, but also builds better relationships with your customers.

9. Create a loyalty and referral program, then track and measure results.

10. Become a trusted advisor.

Here's a tip – you will continue to waste time, energy, and money if you randomly make calls on a list of 5,000. Many names on that list represent different roles within their own company, which means they have different concerns, needs, and problems. Selling to them all in the same manner is the cookie-cutter approach and won't yield very satisfying results.

Gain knowledge and truly understand who is living within your customer list and database. What do they buy and when? Are there identifiable cycles to their spending? Can you see patterns in their buying habits? And are there products you think they should be buying from you but aren't?

Spend some time aligning yourself with your manufacturers to find out who should or could want what you're selling. Talk to your supplier about the trends they are seeing among the buyers overall. Who is more likely to make the purchase within a company? What obstacles are other resellers reporting? Using this information, identify more people who are experiencing the same problems, versus randomly calling on a list of potential customers where problems may vary

Amazon is continually used as an example of great customer marketing on the Web. With each and every visit to this site, you will see something unique to you. Amazon learns its customers' interests through click-through analysis — meaning they pay attention to the products you browse and/or buy. Then Amazon offers similar products they believe you might want. And not only do they show it to you on the site, but they also email you a notice when something of interest is available. And while this is okay for the Web, many appreciate and actually want face-to-face contact with their resellers. This is your opportunity to learn more about your customer, for free!

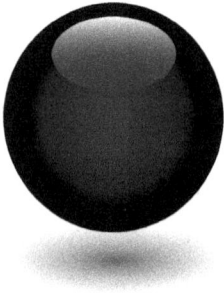

Chapter 3:
Develop Your Database

Do you have days when you scratch your head and have this gut feeling that you're missing sales opportunities with your existing customers? Forget about lead generation and looking for new customers for a moment. Step back and look at the customers you work with, day in and day out. Are you getting the most return on your time with them? Do you know what makes them tick? If not, do you have the resources to find out?

If you answered "yes", then you probably have a good database, or at least one that provides some insight into each of your customers. If not, read on, my friend; we're going to get you started on *the* most important part of your business – a well-oiled machine: an intimate database of *your* customers!

When properly managed, a good database gives you much more than just a list of customers and what they've bought. It speaks volumes about your business. Embedded in this document are clues to new sales opportunities. Are you selling

10 Low-Cost/No-Cost Marketing Ideas

1. Group your customers by common factors, figure out their similar end-user problem, and find the solution.

2. Blog. Write a tip or two every day that offers value to your customers. They'll come back looking for more. And you'll establish yourself as a credible source for information, not just a salesperson.

3. Email a monthly update to your customers, alerting them to upcoming promotions, events, new products and services, and maybe a featured product or service of the month.

4. Project where trends are coming from and then figure out how you can grow with it. You don't have to invent something as revolutionary as the iPod, but you can invent accessories to go with it. Take a profitable ride in the wake of an exciting new trend, product, or technology.

5. Ask your manufacturers for promotional items to use as incentives and feature them into a vertical market? What needs do your customers have? What specific problems are you solving for buyers? The answers are literally at your fingertips – *if* you have a good database. Massage it. Feed and nurture it. Breathe it. Show it some love… every single day.

Start with the Right Software

So where do you start? If you already have a database, great! You can use that file and build upon it. If you don't have one, shop around for off-the-shelf CRM (Customer Relationship Management) software. Don't skimp here. A fancy spreadsheet simply isn't enough, but you don't need to spend a fortune either. Find a system that lets you analyze data according to your organization's specific situation. Look for features that give you the ability to:

- Track customer interactions (phone, fax, email, online, or face-to-face)
- Focus marketing campaigns

as giveaways in your monthly email to your customers.

6. Ideas are brought to life by knowing your customers and end-users, so work your database! Ask your customers one question: What is it you really need but rarely get from your VARs?

7. Find out where your manufacturers are running ads in your area and be sure to piggyback the effort by having them list your name, email, phone, and URL.

8. Use your knowledge of the end user to create specific Web landing pages using their language — and then be sure to drive them there.

9. Submit press releases to the media via the Web. Feature newsworthy (not blatantly promotional) information that end-users will find useful. The fresh content will move you up on the search engines, too!

10. Brainstorm! Come up with ideas and put them into action. With the Internet, you can create a campaign, post it on the Web, and reach out to the world!

(send specific messages to buyer groups about certain products) geared toward customer acquisition, cross-selling or retention

- Monitor sales by product or geographic distribution
- Manage leads, opportunities, and requests for proposals (RFPs)
- Track warranty or service issues
- Spot buying trends
- Pinpoint high-value prospects
- Qualify prospects by interest level, company size, and initial contact method (cold call, advertising, trade show, referral)

Build a Better Database

Now, start by inputting the simplest things you know: your customer's name, contact information, products purchased in the past, buying cycle, any personal information you know about the customer, and any insights the customer has shared with you. For instance, maybe your customer only needs a small supply of computer parts but you know he will be a steady source of orders, month after month. Your customer doesn't have the cash flow to purchase all of them at once, even though he knows he'd receive a better price if he did. You make note of this in your database so that you can provide a valuable service to him – perhaps offering him a payment plan, on-demand pricing, or other solution that makes ordering easy for him and you get the entire sale.

So now you have all this juicy information. What do you do with it? First, identify precisely whom you're selling to, because this knowledge gives you the opportunity to sell your customer other products or services they haven't yet purchased. This method of up-selling and cross-selling is a highly cost-effective way to boost your sales without digging up new leads. Remember, we're only looking at existing customers right now.

Later, after you've mastered your customer database, you can develop a database specific to lead generation if you want.

Listen to your customers' needs and then log them into your database. Note the challenges they face. Having this information at your fingertips will afford you the perfect opportunity to up-sell and cross-sell. Frequently, customers get comfortable buying a certain product and you never think to sell them more than that. But what if you looked into your database and searched beyond what they *think* they need? What if you start offering solutions that subtly up-sell and cross-sell for you? If you keep your database current, you'll have the necessary information about your customer to determine what other products they could use – and your customers will perceive you to be a valuable resource for the latest products and cost-saving solutions for their business.

Why Your Database Will Give You the Competitive Edge

We continue to talk about how a SuperVAR is more than just an order taker. A good VAR brings more to the table for customers than just products that they can purchase. And a good database – one that is current and stores your secret customer information – will show you the path to ensuring that your customers not only continue to buy from you, but also buy *more* from you than they have in the past. Here's where you make yourself stand out among the other resellers. You have this information readily available in your database, and you know your customers' buying trends. Use this information to become a trusted advisor. Help your customers discover why products they have purchased aren't moving and show them how to make improvements to push that inventory. Those are the secrets a good, current database will contain – and those secrets will help you become more profitable!

Of course if you're looking for new customers and you don't even know who your current customers are, how can you possibly find more like them? A database that serves up specific information on existing buyers also pinpoints exactly the type of prospects to target and reveals which approach is likely to work best. Don't let competitors snag a piece of your market while you're chasing "maybes". Work your database to its fullest, keeping abreast of current customer needs while looking for new ones. These two database segments should work in tandem with each other.

Lastly, I offer you one word of advice that's worth its weight in gold – back up your database. Back up, back up, back up! All the information in the world is useless if you lose it, so offsite storage or a redundant backup system is critical. Also, you must maintain your database.

Regularly authenticate contact names and job titles, phone number and addresses – anything that may be outdated. Update the information that you readily have available by making a quick phone call or sending an email to a customer letting them know you're updating your database and want to make sure you have all the correct, up-to-date information about them. This also affords you the opportunity to do a little in-depth questioning too, to really enhance your database information. Or create a small mailer with "Return Service Requested." The invalid addresses bounce back, allowing you to refresh your database. And if it's not worth updating a particular contact, simply delete it or add it to a "revisit" file, a smart investment for any list that has not been updated for two or more years. By tending to your database regularly you'll keep it squeaky clean as well.

Profiling your existing customers and finding new ones that mirror them makes more sense economically than going out to do battle in a new territory with a hot new product, which means you'll need much smaller buckets of money to pay for your advertising collateral!

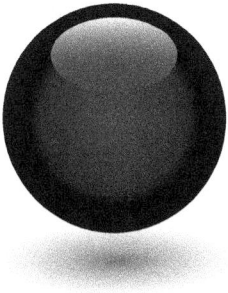

Chapter 4:
Changing Channels: Rethink Your Marketing Options

If you had never-ending cash flow flooding into your business accounts, then you'd never have to actually sit down and analyze which marketing channels are available to you, let alone deciding which options will work best in your specific market segments. But welcome to reality, folks. Marketing budgets are lean and mean these days. You might need to choose between a new sales, technical, or marketing resource. Carefully assessing and applying your financial resources to different channels to achieve the best rate of return is not only important, it's **critical** to the success of your bottom line.

Times have changed. Not long ago, a postcard mailing or a telemarketing campaign may have raked in sales. While those techniques can still serve some of your specific functions, we're in a whole new world, marketing-wise. And in today's rapid-fire marketplace, technology and all of its "rewards" have us moving at blistering speed – and that includes those customers you're trying to reach. "Don't blink or you'll miss it." That's the way your customers may feel when they're viewing some of your marketing as well as that of your competitors. Companies are sponsoring major events – and even the stadiums where they take place like The Fleet Center, Coors Field, Gillette Stadium, and U.S. Cellular Field, just to name a few. With texting, email, ezines, pay-per-click advertising, and other media supplanting traditional ad venues, you've got more to think about when planning your marketing mix.

To be successful today, you must cultivate the many tools and media you have available to create your own custom blend – in other words, a "marketing mix" that zeroes in on your customers and their specific needs and desires. We've talked about not just thinking *outside* the box, but actually burning the box. And while traditional media like print, radio, direct mail, and telemarketing are still valuable tools, more and more you'll need to customize those tools to complement the many uses of the Internet (I'll talk about a few here, but really delve into a complete website and Internet discussion in the next chapter). Think of your unique marketing mix like a cup of gourmet coffee. It might require a little more effort and thinking on your part to get your custom mix right, but the reward is far richer than the ordinary brew.

Preparing Your Marketing Mix

To blend your initial marketing mix, start by making a list of all the options available to you, like direct mail, email, online, telemarketing, trade shows, advertising, and publicity. Be specific. Make the Internet one category, as a way to drive traffic to your site. Then put website as another topic, so you place the necessary emphasis on tending to your valuable site and not letting it stagnate.

Next to each category, list specific actions to use each method. Make another column where you will identify both the cost of the effort and the desired return. This will help you evaluate the best use of your marketing dollars.

To determine your ideal combination, start by mirroring the mindset of the people you want to reach. If they are mostly Internet-savvy customers adept at collecting information and making comparisons online, you need to provide easy access to the information they want — or risk losing sales. If they still value a face-to-face interaction, be ready to accommodate those preferences in your mix.

Then ask yourself how your customers get their information. Are they reading trade journals? If so, print ads might make sense. Do they get their news online? Banner ads or sponsorship opportunities might be the way to go for that customer segment. Are the actual buyers seeing direct mail pieces or is someone filtering it for them? If that's the case (and it often is), your postcards might not be reaching your target market. Do you know which trade shows your customers attend? Look into sponsorship opportunities or vendor exhibits. And what about the many ways you can use technology and the Internet to boost sales? The choices for your mix are literally endless and creating your own marketing mix is not difficult. Simply give your customers what they want, how and when they want it. Do that and sales will escalate.

Ingredients in the Mix

Let's take a few minutes to review the traditional marketing channels – those familiar methods that are most often discussed in marketing textbooks.

Print – As I mentioned, depending on what your customers are reading for publications these days, traditional print or display ads may be a viable way to connect with your customers. The trick is to determine those customers who are still reading traditional publications versus the ones who are viewing news and information online. If the latter seems to comprise the bulk of your customers, put more marketing dollars into Internet advertising. Also, examine the various publications within a specific genre.

Your customers may pore through a trade magazine specific to their products and needs versus a more traditional consumer magazine that talks more to your customers' end users. Depending on the circulation, the trade publication's display ad rates are probably less expensive than a consumer magazine. You may not reach as vast a number of readers, but you're hitting a much more targeted audience — hitting the bullseye and ideally yielding better return on your ad dollars.

Broadcast – Product placement has taken over large chunks of the television ad budget so, depending on the marketing dollars you have to spend and how concentrated each of your target markets is, traditional broadcast media (including radio) may just be cost prohibitive. However, as you stomp "the box," you'll see that there are other ways of being seen. For instance, tap into the resources of your local cable channel. By law, cable TV is required to give access to people to create their own shows or infomercials (via local cable access networks). After being trained to use the equipment they loan you, you can create your own Cable TV show, complete with the questions and answers that *you* want to use and the guests *you'd* like to host. Call on some of your most valuable customers or end-users who are willing to offer insight into trends in the industry. Make them the experts. In doing so, you not only showcase your business, but provide value-added service to your customers who gain from the exposure. Being creative with available broadcast options can provide you with a powerful message using minimal financial resources.

Direct Mail – If you segment your database into meaningful categories (which they already should be!), you can create a targeted direct mail campaign using one or a series of postcards or mailers with specific messaging to your target categories. How many customers bought from you in the last year? Two years? Look at the list. Then craft your message according to who bought what and when. Create an incentive and call to action on the postcard that drives them to your website or toll-free number. You may even want to send out a reminder about an important trade show, where your booth will be located, and a "show special" that you're running this month on a specific product you know a particular group of customers will want. You can also get more creative with direct mail to get attention. If your message is about innovation, create a package with something unique in a box that links to a specific message and a compelling call to action. Try a mailer in a unique shape (a light bulb), a mailer with sound, or a "pop-up" card. Mailers can grab their attention in a new way using an "old" marketing mix element. The downfall? Expense. Between design, printing, and postage costs, you may well exceed your budget without a good sense of your response rate. As always, look at past response rates to similar campaigns to evaluate their effectiveness. If it worked, go for it. If it didn't, try another option in your marketing mix.

Telemarketing – Telemarketing is one way to speak one-on-one with customers, but, let's face it, *no one* likes to get those calls. But don't cross this medium off your list without considering the opportunity to up-sell or cross-sell your customers using telemarketing. If you offer a specific group of customers a "free trial" to something of value, your campaign may have some legs. You can use this campaign to position yourself as a valuable resource who is looking out for the needs of the customer by extending this special offer. But, before you pick up that phone, be sure to really assess the time involved to craft the language, make the call, and pay the phone bill.

The Internet – The catch-all word "Internet" can be divided into so many categories. There's a good chance that most of your marketing dollars are probably best spent in this category. I like to consider the Internet in many ways – your own personal website (up next in Chapter 5), free and not-so-free advertising on the Internet, email marketing, ezines, blogs, podcasts, webinars, article marketing, maximum utilization of search engine rankings, and optimizing your own website. With ever-changing technology and more and more people spending most of their time on the Web, opportunities abound, many of which are free, or just about.

Don't forget that this is *your* marketing mix. You must create a combination of elements with *your* website as the anchor, to help reinforce *your* message to *your* target audience. One item alone won't help you achieve your objective. Each element must link to the overall campaign or initiative. One focused message should be integrated and reinforced in every element of your campaign. Finally, measure your results. Try to determine if one of the tactics is generating more results more effectively and then shift your campaign investment into that area.

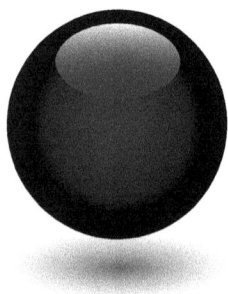

Chapter 5:
Unraveling the Web

I know this is the chapter you've been anxious to skip ahead to – Web and Internet marketing! I'm proud of you for getting through the important first chapters. Now we're going to take a look at where much of your marketing dollars **should** be invested. I'll also show you how to maximize low-cost or free opportunities, both with your website as well as on the Internet. Ready?

First, let's look inward and delve into your website. Successful companies are tuned into the hyper-speed needs and wants of today's consumer – the Nanosecond consumer. The one who's demanding the fastest Internet access possible, wireless capabilities to work anytime, anywhere, and 24/7 access to anything, anywhere, thanks to a Bluetooth, iPhone, or Blackberry. There's no need to return a phone call; consumers just send a quick text or instant message. They shop online in their slippers to find the most obscure products at any hour of the day, which they then want (and expect) to arrive tomorrow, because time is precious. So your overall marketing strategy should include a strong online presence. But please, don't just "throw up" a website — any more than you would whip together an ad or direct mail campaign. Put some thought into your site to maximize this powerful marketing tool which can generate more leads and close more deals.

K.I.S.S. – Keep It Simple, Stupid

Okay, I know you're not stupid. That's why you're here, reading this guide! The K.I.S.S. approach is an age-old reminder that you shouldn't over-complicate your message, offer, or the means for grabbing the sale. Instead, develop a streamlined website that delivers all the information that consumers hungrily devour in the easiest manner possible. Then, make it brilliantly simple to close the deal. Forget the bells and whistles.

Go for function over Flash. Add a podcast or two – they're easy and effective. But, above all, give your customers what they want, and make it easy and natural for them to find it on your site. Then keep your website fresh with updates that will make visitors want to keep coming back. And, **please**, included a "Contact Us" link on every page. After all, you want your customers to contact you, so make it easy for them to do so — or they'll move on to someone else they can reach.

With the Internet, it's easier than ever to create "customized" sites with unique offers and messages, and then instantly change or update the sites when new information is available. You'll be a thought leader, someone your customers turn to for a fresh perspective and whom they will turn to for purchasing choices.

Generating Leads from the Web

Not only does your website help sell your products and services, it also can easily generate new leads for you – from either existing customers or new visitors to your site. So, once visitors land at your site, you need to grab hold and keep them there — as willing and eager participants who gladly serve up information on themselves. Podcasts and blogs are a creative, effective, and inexpensive way to engage new visitors. One powerful way to produce these, and capitalize on word-of-mouth marketing at the same time, is to ask your customers to create a podcast or short video for your site. Consumer-Generated Advertising (CGA) has become a popular method for consumers to gain notoriety and the advertiser to get interesting, creative and inexpensive ads. You'll want to be involved in writing the scripts so their story addresses the issue(s) your customer faced and how your company provided a smart solution. Or, you can record your own video or audio to explain what your company has done for customers and explain how you can repeat that success story for them. From there, direct them to the contact us page and capture their information, including an area for them to explain what *their* problems are.

Your page ranking can also have a big influence on driving new leads. If you rank in the top three of a Google search, for example, chances are that new visitor is going to click on that ranking, versus a paid "sponsorship" link at the top or on the right. The page ranking provides more credibility for a new visitor than that of a paid (sponsored) ad, which they often ignore. The concept is similar to the fact that free publicity (like an article in a newspaper) garners more believability than a paid display ad in that same newspaper.

Remember, ideas are brought to life by knowing your end user and this holds true for your website's visitors. Seek out their problems, needs, and desires, and then develop a website that delivers on that. You will soon become the invaluable resource they seek out time after time — and one they refer to others as well

10 Ways to Maximize Your Website's Value

1. **Look professional.** Your online presence reflects your identity and your corporate image. Don't delude yourself into thinking you're wisely saving marketing dollars by taking shortcuts with mediocre website design (which includes the content and navigation as well as the visual). This "bargain" can cost you more than it saves. But you don't want to spend a fortune either. Look at the sites of competitors or others that you like for their clean, clear

design. Then find out who the designers are. Get a few design quotes then make your decision based on what the designer can provide you at a reasonable cost.

2. **Differentiate yourself.** This website is your platform to tell the world who you are and why you should be the chosen one. Include on your site the value proposition that's reflected in your other marketing collateral. Your website should reinforce your existing messages and help to set you apart from the crowd.

3. **Keep it simple.** I've already talked about this but it's worth repeating. While all the animation and Flash tricks look fun, they can be very cumbersome and frustrating to the end users, possibly pushing them to make a hasty departure from your site. A really cool intro can just be an annoyance to a visitor who wants to get right to the meat of your site. Your site should include the basics, like a top masthead and either horizontal or vertical navigation bar. Each page should be clear in its information. Build your site by thinking as a new or beginner user would, keeping things easy and familiar.

4. **Add fresh content.** You want your customers to keep coming back to your site because they know you are the expert who understands their business problems. As I always say, give them what they want and solve their problems! Keep your site fresh with new content – not new design – like trend-centered articles, ideas, or briefs that are meaningful to your visitors. Search engines also

look for fresh content on a regular basis, so this will help with your search engine optimization as well, garnering higher rankings. Consider creating a site map and include its access on your homepage. You may have customers with very different needs, and with a site map, you can "help" your new visitor navigate to the pages that matter most to him. This way, your potential new customers find information specific to *their* needs versus more general information. You have provided useful information and gently directed them through the site to where *you* want them to go. This ideally leads to a faster conversion rate from visitor to registered user to buyer.

5. **Track visitor activity.** Most hosts will provide some sort of tracking mechanism to monitor your site so you can determine who is visiting your site, for how long, the number of pages visited, and which ones. This data will tell you where you have strong content that is maintaining reader interest, which pages need work, and how visitors find your site. Google Analytics is a free service that can show you visitor trends, high traffic pages, and more. Other paid services like WebTrends Analytics, OneStat.com, or StatCounter offer even more in-depth stats and reports, depending on how deep you want to go. But remember, analytics are only as good as their frequency of use. You must set aside some time (each week, month, etc.) to review your reports and then adjust your website and tactics accordingly.

6. **Bring the TV generation to your website.** Webinars

(conferences on the Web), podcasts (typically an audio file), and screen capture demonstrations (video files, usually of software applications) are some of the short, but powerful, images that turn browsers into buyers when visiting your site. Visit a few sites of interest to you and see what they're doing with these little extras. Imagine if your customer could automatically download your latest podcast or webinar right to their MP3 player and listen to it on the way to work? What a way to get in their heads!

7. **Add purpose to your pages.** Map out each page with the desired response from the visitor. Every page should make a logical contribution to the whole site and drive the visitor to become a registered user and then a buyer. When planning your navigation, ask yourself what you want each individual page to accomplish. Do you want the visitor to click through to another page? Do you want them to send a request for a quote? Keep this in mind and make it simple for them to follow your lead.

8. **Connect with visitors.** Newsletters are a great way to keep your name in front of customers and prospects. Include a sign-up (opt-in) link on your site that is enticing enough to extract their contact information so you can add it to your database. Consider creating a blog (web log) as an extension of your site, since they are highly favored by search engines. These online journals can be very brief (just a few sentences) and touch on topics of interest to your visitors. Plus, you get the added advantage of fresh content on a regular basis, which is the nectar of the search

engine gods! The fresher your content, the higher your page ranking.

9. **Have a contingency plan.** What happens if your site goes down because your host's (either your or an outside service provider's) server goes down? Or what if you have an amazing response to an offer and don't have enough bandwidth to handle it? Make sure your IT manager takes the necessary steps to manage unforeseen events.

10. **Offer a shopping cart.** If you have product that can be purchased instantly, give your customers that option with a simple shopping cart. Remember, these folks are online at all hours of the day. No need to lose a sale simply because someone wants to make a purchase at 1 a.m. or if you're on Eastern time and someone is ordering from California on Pacific time.

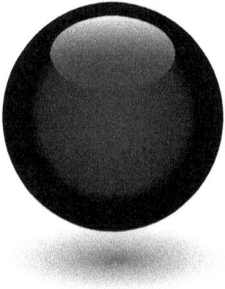

Chapter 6:
Plan for Success

These past five chapters have given you the simple, straightforward ways to market yourself and your products at little or no cost. Now, what are *you* going to do with them?

You need a plan — a good, solid marketing plan that will provide a blueprint for your company's activities and initiatives for the coming year. I know, you're pumped up and ready to get started *now* — building your database, spending more time with your customers, placing some ads, creating new partnerships — but just hold on a minute!

Let's talk about some of the benefits of establishing, implementing, and maintaining a marketing plan. You wouldn't book a trip to Paris without researching the best-valued hotels, would you? Would you reserve your plane ticket only? Would you give your accommodations a low priority on your "to do" list, figuring you'd just "find something" when you arrive? Hopefully you would walk into that situation knowing that you'd probably either pay premium prices for a luxurious room or a cheap price that clearly states, "You get what you pay for."

Poor planning doesn't just apply to your vacation plans; it goes for your business and marketing plans, too. What if you took the same approach to creating your new website that you did to plan the Paris trip? You would either pay top dollar because some fantastic designer sold you the whole package, complete with all the bells and whistles that you really don't need (remember Chapter 5?), or you went for a budget package that uses standard, templated design for creating sites, where there's no room for growth, navigation is a bear, and you have no control over updating content. Either way, you've now negatively impacted your bottom line – all because you didn't spend a bit of time upfront, creating your strategy for success.

What Does a Great Marketing Plan Accomplish?

All plans are not created equal. Your marketing plan should make you think strategically about your business and how you want to succeed. It will help you prioritize projects according to importance, milestones, and significant events. Your plan will help you identify your market — who they are, where they are, what they need — and then focus your thinking on the strategy for reaching them, This blueprint will also help you to estimate the costs for each activity. Create a calendar as part of this plan to see the big picture and establish timelines to make yourself and your employees accountable for reaching certain goals. Also, by scheduling events like trade shows, product launches, and editorial deadlines well in advance, you can create synergies among various marketing channels to work effectively, efficiently, and within budget. And, of course, to reap positive results.

The Marketing Assessment

The marketing assessment is perhaps the most crucial element of any marketing plan. This step directs you to evaluate your company's presence in the market, its position relation to its competitors, and its products against competitive products. While developing the assessment, make sure to evaluate:

- **Current marketing methods** – Identify and then list all existing ways you market and sell products and services, including print advertisements, direct mailings, sales support, telemarketing, trade shows, public relations, Internet marketing, and websites.

- **Sales response to marketing efforts** – Evaluate success of marketing activities, including the number of responses to ads, number of booth inquiries at trade shows, number of page views on the company Web site, average number of sales calls necessary to close sales, and response to PR and press publications.

- **Recommended changes** – Determine the weaknesses of the marketing program, including ineffective ads, inadequate presentation in marketing collateral, inaccurate database information (such as wrong addresses or contacts), poor marketing execution (including missed deadlines or production errors) or bad allocation of the marketing budget.

- **Future marketing events** – Identify upcoming events, such as trade shows, product launches, sales promotions, and editorial deadlines.

- **Efforts required for upcoming initiatives** – Determine the support and deliverables necessary for scheduled marketing projects and events.

- **Industry and market developments** – Identify market trends and conditions, pricing pressures, and changes in regulations and industry standards. For example, a stagnant or declining market typically warrants more aggressive marketing efforts, while a booming industry suggests the opposite. Price drops in the overall market may indicate the need for changes in the company's distribution structure and a corresponding change in the marketing plan. Changes in standards

and regulations may present exciting new marketing
opportunities.

- **Competitor analysis** – Assess competitors' strengths
  and weaknesses, reputation in the industry, and how
  they market their products.

Determine Your Marketing Budget

I know it sounds crazy and I may be overstating the obvious, but you
must have a budget before you can leverage your marketing mix. Do
not simply dive in, spending on a whim because "it feels right" or "it's
worked for me before." Determine the importance of each marketing
channel, then allocate dollars accordingly. Typically, a company's overall
marketing budget may be determined by one of the following methods:

- Spend roughly the same amount each year, based on
  proven market activities and adjust that amount up or
  down, as necessary;

- Observe competitors' marketing programs and
  combine this data with information available in their
  market to arrive at an industry standard figure; or

- Allocate a fixed percentage of projected yearly revenue
  on marketing and sales.

You have to choose – literally pick – what will be your true path to
success. Putting an effective marketing plan in place is the best strategy
to walk along your path as a winner. Even though it may look like it or
we think they do, artists just don't throw paint on paper. They plan their
art by mapping out the colors they want to use, envisioning the type of

image to create, and choosing the brush style (or other tool). Where does it make sense to put your energy to get the most success? Don't be afraid to put your ideas down on paper and then design a plan to make them work. Just look at how the iPod has changed the music industry!

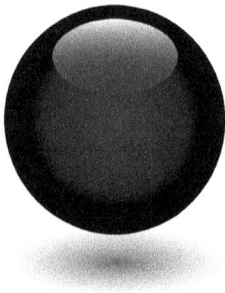

Chapter 7:
Measure Your Progress

Now, you've got all these great ideas and you're off and running with them – congratulations! But the journey isn't over yet. In order for you to be truly successful, I now charge you with the task of figuring of what worked, what didn't, and then tweaking your plan accordingly. It's an ongoing process – you are fine-tuning your craft **and** your business.

Hopefully, by now, you've determined your true business objective(s). Do you need more business? Do you want to be successful? Great, join the club! But what does "successful" really mean to you? "I want to be successful" is not a measurable goal. If you don't have a goal or objective that can stand up to measurement, you can never determine your degree of success. You can say you want to increase sales and if you do that by just one dollar, then you've succeeded. But was that minor achievement really your intention? Why not raise the bar and declare, "I will increase my sales by 14%"?

How Do You Know What Works?

Measuring your tactics and your initiatives will be the most effective way for you to learn what worked and what didn't. For instance, if you want to increase *awareness* of your brand or a specific product or service that you offer, does it really matter to you if it's measurable or not? Probably not. As another example, some companies invest in real estate space on billboards, also known as outdoor advertising. Billboards are expensive and for obvious reasons, very hard to measure. How many impressions does any single billboard create? Sure, you can estimate how many cars drive by but how many of those drivers and passengers match your target audience? And was that billboard used to introduce or reinforce your brand or sell a specific product? The marketing manager may argue that the billboards were very effective because sales went up. But technically there is no direct correlation to prove that!

Let's look at one example where an ad agency actually put together an outdoor advertising campaign around a fictitious brand. Called "Outhouse Springs," this recycled water didn't exist. An ad agency created a fictitious product and then promoted the odd beverage on billboards. But the ad campaign was so bizarre that people took note. Those in the community where the billboards were situated actually started looking for Outhouse Springs water in their local stores. Because there was so much demand, the agency partnered with a vendor to produce the water! And, they donated part of the proceeds of the water to a local charitable foundation. Turning a fake brand into a new one based on demand — *that* is success!

Balancing Creativity With Results

Audiences are looking for creative thinkers and they appreciate entertainment in advertising. But creativity still must have a source of measurement. For instance, an award-winning ad campaign, while creative, slick and beautiful to look at and read, may not actually influence your sales efforts or impact your bottom line. Was the money well spent? Maybe. The ad campaign obviously was recognizable since it won awards. But did it have financial impact? How many times have you told someone about a great commercial you enjoyed, only to add, "I forget who the ad was for but it was fantastic!"? Yes, it was fun for the viewer but not for the anonymous advertiser. Your tactics should always have a clear, concise message. Just because you don't have tens of thousands of dollars to throw at a creative branding campaign doesn't mean you can't spend time developing the way to tell your story. It's the poignancy of your message that matters – not the splash!

Great ideas *are* free, but what is the difference between receiving something that's good, better, or the absolute best? It's really just the little things that make the difference between average and exceptional. Create a campaign that creatively delivers your message to a specific targeted group of customers. But make sure it's measurable. Creative thinking is not expensive, but it does require you to shift your mindset.

Be creative in your ideas and your methods. Find a way to get your message across to your market segment *and* to measure the response. And then, if a campaign doesn't work, try something else. BUT, always, always evaluate what you did. Maybe you did it wrong. Or maybe some of it worked and you just need to tweak it a bit more and try it on a different group.

There are loads of calculators and templates out there to measure your marketing's effectiveness. Here's an example of a template to help measure effectiveness:

Back-of-the-Napkin Model

A. Cost of tactic	$5,000	
B. # of responses	2,500	
C. Cost per response	$2.00 (A divided by B)	
D. # who purchased	75	
E. % who purchased	3% (D divided by B)	
F. Cost per customer	$66.67 (A divided by D)	

With this type of hard data, you can determine both the success of specific campaigns and your sales goals. Did the $66.67 cost per customer provide a breakeven point for you? What would it take for your sales force to have boosted the closure rate? Your marketing and sales efforts need to work together. Keep them as a team. The job of marketing is to draw interest; your sales people are in charge of closing the deals. Be clear about the roles of each and give them each a set of measurable goals.

It is critical that you make sure you're on the right track with your efforts; otherwise, you will simply spin your wheels, waste precious time, and, most importantly, waste money. *Marketing can and should be measured.* Measurement milestones allow you to check your progress and adjust your efforts, as needed. Ultimately, one of your goals should be for all your marketing campaigns to be successful and measurable.

Bottom line – as you design your marketing action, think about what you are asking your customers to do, what results would you consider successful, and what means you will use to measure the campaign. Take a look at these ways to measure your efforts:

- Use your web analytics reports to track the number of (1) "hits" to your campaign's URL; or (2) request for information forms on your website for downloading a white paper, executive summary, or podcasts.

- Monitor the number of end users who request the specific item that you are offering. Compare the number of sales to the number of days the offer was available to your customers.

- Use your email distribution system to track: (1) unique "opens" on your email blasts; or (2) the number of new contacts you reach via email forwarding. Did those new contacts register for your newsletter and/or request or download your product or offer? If not, find out why!

- Keep track of who attends your special event or webinar; of those people, who asked for a quote or a follow-up visit/call? Did you get referrals from those who attended, and if so, how many?

- If you use direct mail, insert a special code people can use to request material or a special offer (10% off their next order over $500). Be sure to track the code when customers respond.

- Consider utilizing a special 800 number for phone responses. Track the number of inbound calls to this number from the campaign.

- Utilize personalization to automate the creation, management, and tracking of Personalized URLs and VIP Landing Pages. The result? You'll convert more direct mail recipients into qualified prospects and valued customers. This easy step provides a unique one-to-one communication with your customers and a great tracking method.

Summary

Now that you've read this book, you may be wondering if everything you've read is just ideas. You may be thinking, "Do people really use these ideas and do they work?" The answer is a resounding YES!

I talked a lot about the importance of your database and regular customer contact, treating your best customers uniquely and differently. I've done it. And continue to do it. I update my database constantly, sending "thank you" notes with customer specific information, emailing monthly offers to my database, and over time, have had a regular stream of customers who have bought specifically and exclusively from me as a result of these extra — **and free** — efforts.

Today, customers are more powerful than ever before. They actually "own" the power. The Internet gives them access to it all; they learn more and they learn faster. They have data immediately at their fingertips. New brands can pop up overnight, become a trend and an instantaneous hit. Traditional brands and marketing models are no longer the norm. Today, marketers can test new ideas in the marketplace and get almost instant feedback and results – virtually for free! Business owners communicate globally on a daily basis. Everything is available in a click.

To support the world of continuous change or to seek out new, unique opportunities – test ideas. Test campaigns, offers, and packages on pieces of your market. Develop a concept and ask your "advisory" group about it or send out your concept to a small segment of your database. Then try a different approach with a different segment and see which concept is more compelling. Which one has a better rate of return? With the Internet, it's cheaper, faster, and far less risky to experiment than ever before. And — let me say it one more time — it's free!

Post this quick checklist to keep yourself on track as you build your plan:

1. Remember, marketing is your job and you must be involved and engaged in the process for your business to be successful. Great marketing affects your bottom line. Figure out what you're missing in your plan, and then get to work on patching that hole.

2. Put on your psychologist's hat and get inside your customers' heads – get to know them intimately, understand what makes them tick – or ticked off – and find ways to help solve their problems using your resources and products. You'll find a customer for life if you can anticipate and address their needs before they do.

3. Mine your database daily and know what your customers want, when they want it and how often. And for goodness sake, if you don't have a database, or started one a few years ago but haven't touched it since, please build one – NOW. This is *the* most important part of your business!

4. Rethink your marketing options and develop a marketing mix that works for you and your business. In today's fast-paced world, what may have worked yesterday to draw in business could easily be obsolete tomorrow. Did a print ad garner a high volume of phone calls? Maybe if it didn't, a specifically targeted email campaign may have produced better results. Finding

that creative mix will be key as your business and marketing plans continue to evolve.

5. Keep your website clean, simple, and professional, and please make sure it's easy to navigate. While there are beautiful bells and whistles out there like Flash, anyone who is still on dial-up or can't get to the information they want will quickly leave your site – a customer you most likely have lost forever. Once your site is live, seek out ways to utilize all the free opportunities on the Internet. Start a blog, use email marketing with links to specific pages on your site, and capture information on new leads from a "contact us" form or other type of feedback mechanism. The ideas are endless here.

6. Create a great marketing plan. Figure out where you can be most successful and then focus your energies on generating ideas to support those areas. Put your ideas on paper and build a plan (or plans) around them. Create a budget for smart-business checks and balances. Then get to it!

7. Create ways to measure your successes – or to learn where your not-so-successful plans or projects missed their mark. Without benchmarks and ways to evaluate and measure your progress, you will never know how you are really doing. You could be just spinning your wheels. Learn what worked and what didn't and continue to tweak your plan. It's an ongoing process based on the changing needs of your customers and your business.

Great marketing *is* free. These ideas really do work. Just remember it's a fast-paced world out there today. "Research, plan, do" is the old mantra. Today's is "do, do, do." By using some of these ideas, you *will* make a difference. It might not be instantaneous and you might need to do some testing and changing of tactics and offers – and yes, it will require some hard work. But it **will** make a difference for you and your business in the long run. Good luck!

A dedicated marketing professional, Michelle Kabele has been helping technology companies develop award-winning channel partner programs and marketing strategies for over 10 years. Her innovative channel marketing concepts have been adopted and implemented by many leading technology companies, including Zebra Technologies, 3Com Corporation and U.S. Robotics. Moreover, Michelle has worked extensively with VARs throughout North America and thoroughly understands the realities and practicalities they face in planning and executing effective promotional, marketing, and sales campaigns.

Michelle has an MBA from the J.L. Kellogg Graduate School of Management (Evanston, Ill.) and an undergraduate degree from Northwestern University (Evanston, Ill.)

For more great ways to build your business, check out Michelle Kabele's other books:

All the Web's A Stage: How to Make Your Business A Hit on the Internet
50 Smart, Easy and Effective Ideas to Boost Your Business Today
Just Say "Yes!": The Power of Creative Thinking Outside That Tired Old Box
The Pocket Guide to Marketing Speak: Stop Mouthing the Words and Start Using Them

Visit www.ideastormpress.com for the most up-to-the-minute news, advice, ideas, and just cool stuff.